I0432356

MENTES

LIBRES

PASSIVE INCOME

PASSIVE INCOME

The *revolution* for *freedom*

PASSIVE INCOME

 PASSIVE INCOME

INDEX

We begin

What is passive income

Use of residual income

Use of leveraged revenue

Using Leveraged Active Income

Use of Internet Marketing

Use of network marketing

Use of Real Estate

Use of blogs

Set goals and have a plan

The mentality necessary for a passive income

Final thoughts

 PASSIVE INCOME

We begin

Any income where the individual does not have to physically earn is called passive income. This is, of course, a very attractive way of earning income and, in fact, those who are lucky enough to earn a living this way are very happy.

The move to passive income

Generate truck loads of passive income and live the four working hours of the week

 PASSIVE INCOME

What is passive income

There are now some very popular and common ways to earn passive income. Writing a new tune or song or even a jingle and selling it as commercial property will generate very lucrative passive income. Opening a bank savings account is another way to get the individual to save money and get some kind of residual interest although it is not much and often fluctuates at the whim and fantasy of banking systems.

Learn the basics

Starting a multi-level business is another way to generate passive income. There are some multi-level companies that do not require the standard job of recruiting and selling products, but only using their products. Becoming a financial products consultant is not only a good passive source of income, but also a way to broaden the customer base.

 PASSIVE INCOME

For those who have a little more money to spare, they can consider other types of investments that are likely to generate profits. Buying a property and renting it helps the person repay the loan, so it does not require an immediate financial commitment.

There are many innovative ways to make money with the Internet engine. All it takes is a little time to look for legitimate business tools. One of the most popular tools is creating your own information for e-books and other online selling tools that perhaps require language changes. The riskiest way to obtain passive income would be to invest in various stocks and bonds. However, the levels of risk are quite high and often not worthwhile.

PASSIVE INCOME

Use of residual income

After all monthly commitments have been paid, the money left over is known as residual income. This income can be of great help to an individual and is usually linked to the more established income group. This is

 PASSIVE INCOME

also how the banking sector calculates the probability of granting a loan commitment to its clients. This is an income that also continues to give well beyond the time frame of the first down payment.

What's left over

There are many ways to try to get residual income. Writing, for example, is a way to venture into this field of earning residual income.

If writing material is good there would be an opportunity to sell the rights, and so it is with other ways like writing a viable software program, composing a song, inventing a gadget and many more.

 PASSIVE INCOME

Become famous as perhaps an actor or singer, where you still get paid every time you reuse work you've done before. When this is done for other modes of entertainment, the artist gets a residual income in the form of certain percentages of the original initial performance.

Obtaining residual income from real estate is perhaps one of the most popular styles of investment with this intention in mind. If you do well this type of residual income in the most ideal and profitable.

Other much simpler ways of earning residual income would include starting a savings plan at an early age. Maintaining this diligently would help ensure a comfortable retirement

 PASSIVE INCOME

in which residual income would be of great help.

The best types of residual income plans are typically those in which the individual had complete autonomy over how, where and when the product is used. By being able to dictate the methods of use, the individual also has the final say on how the general promotion and other aspects of the invention go.

 PASSIVE INCOME

Use of leveraged revenue

This is perhaps one of the most beneficial ways to create the possibility of having a continuous income in a long-term scenario.

Using the leveraged income style, the

individual earns more money with much less effort simply because the gains made are not only the direct result of one's own efforts, but also from the added sources of other people's efforts.

Using

Ideally, most people work to try to earn this kind of income both in the short term and in the long term. In its most basic terms, leverage income allows the individual to concentrate on other efforts once the initial stages of creating and implementing a particular project have begun. This project is then left to generate income without the need for any further particular daily commitments on the part of the investor or inventor.

 PASSIVE INCOME

Most people who feel financially comfortable have ventured into this type of investment, with the intention of generating some kind of leveraged income.

Using a little time and effort to do a project and then taking a step back as the project finally executes itself is, in fact, the perfect scenario.

Therefore, this style of leveraging purchasing power gives the individual the option of retiring early and enjoying the fruits of their labor without the hassle of having to supervise the raid or having to be physically involved.

In addition to the various investment arms that can be used to generate leveraged

PASSIVE INCOME

income, starting a network marketing or business enterprise is also another of the most popular ways to generate this style of income.

This, of course, requires some hard work at first, but once the business is established; there will no longer be any need to be as involved as in the initial stages.

PASSIVE INCOME

Using Leveraged Active Income

Active leveraged income operates on more or less the same principles as the normal leveraged income format, with one

 PASSIVE INCOME

significant distinction.

In this style, the individual will be required to be more practical and to have a greater percentage of participation in the initial stage and at some stagnant stage throughout the incursion.

Action

The fact of being able to offer a service or product that "continues to give" on a large scale would, of course, be ideal, so the study of a product or service of this type can give rise to some quite interesting and viable options.

Some of the simple options of active

leveraged revenue would include servicing conferences and workshop seminars. It is also beneficial to conduct training sessions for companies, as the material used would already have been designed as a basic format to be used over and over again with only a few adjustments being made from time to time.

Designing good home study modules is also another very cost effective way of obtaining the leveraged income style to earn a comfortable living. This also requires an initial investment of time and effort that normally creates the platform for continuous and profitable revenue streams. By doing so, it allows the individual to focus on other possible forays to further improve the income base.

PASSIVE INCOME

The most successful formulas used in the past only required the individual to concentrate on designing a product or service that would be used and reused continuously and consistently, thus creating the desired income that would eventually become leveraged income.

There are basically three types of leveraged revenue styles. The active leverage style, the passive leverage style and the basic leverage style.

All your style requires some initial work, but if designed and executed well, the hand of long-term participation can be kept to a minimum.

PASSIVE INCOME

Use of Internet Marketing

Internet marketing is also referred to by several other terms such as digital marketing, web marketing, online marketing, search marketing, and e marketing. All of them have a similar marketing style with only a small difference, but all have the main intention of making money.

The Network

This style of marketing is considered quite broad and lucrative.

This style may include services such as creative and technical assistance, design, development, advertising and sales. The various possible services that the Internet marketing tool can provide include the customer's interactive engagement, a search engine provider for marketing purposes, an ad platform, and many other possible earning tools.

 PASSIVE INCOME

The use of the Internet marketing tool can provide a one-to-one approach that is not always possible in the "real" world scenario.

This approach, although quite broad and without a particular direction, can be achieved through the use of keywords that are entered by the user in order to obtain the required information or service.

The design of marketing tools that are supposed to attract specific interest groups is also done through the Internet marketing route.

This style created the platform for the connections that must be made between a typical group of segments and the promoted product.

 PASSIVE INCOME

Niche marketing done through the Internet marketing tool has its merits. The success of the style is very successful and is certainly popular among those who have limited time and interest to surf the Internet. Therefore, this service provided is very beneficial for them and widely used as well.

The advantages of creating an Internet marketing business have many advantages, ranging from the possible large revenues derived from the leisure rhythm that one can dictate. However, nothing, of course, comes without a certain level of effort to see the desired success and being the most common business tool now, well worth the effort to investigate.

PASSIVE INCOME

Use of network marketing

It is a form of person-to-person marketing, there is a real need for people to go out and look for customers who may be interested in the products being sold. This method is used when it is considered better than obtaining any business through other methods such as offline and online marketing tools. Here the use of independent representatives is the key to the success of the business venture.

Networking

Recruitment campaigns are often carried out to try to get people to become individual agents or promoters of a company. Some of these companies follow multi-level marketing styles, while others only need to identify potential distributors.

Using network marketing to create residual income is another way to provide a more comfortable life from a financial angle. This way of earning is done at your own pace and commitment. Basically, the more you work, the better your chances of earning more residual income. The individual also has the privilege of deciding with whom and when

 PASSIVE INCOME

to conduct any business.

This is a very important aspect for some people who enjoy meeting and making new friends while gaining the advantage of an extra source of income.

This method also often involves very little monetary investment and no long-term commitment. The reason most people choose to try their hand at network marketing is because of the very lucrative promise of a residual income perspective.

Seeing the success of others who have achieved a comfortable financial status is a good benchmark for focusing on the pursuit of a person's own ambitions for a good and healthy residual income.

Another interesting thing to keep in mind is that there is no age limit for this type of effort.

PASSIVE INCOME

Use of Real Estate

This is another way to create residual income without having to limit yourself too much to a particular style or commitment requirement.

The demand for real estate to create residual income is rapidly gaining popularity as the

 PASSIVE INCOME

success rate and remunerations can be quite tempting.

Real estate

Some of the "pull" factors include the ability to control the levels reached in terms of income earned. Quotas are rarely set or agents are forced to meet them.

However, for some real estate agents who are linked to certain companies there are several incentive programs that are put in place to help generate the momentum to push agents to higher performance standards.

Creating one's own personal security with residual income from the sale of real estate is

 PASSIVE INCOME

also another attractive reason to venture into this endeavor. The income derived from this particular type of residual income is definitely worth working toward an early retirement plan.

When making the decision to venture into the real estate style of earning residual income, the feeling of being able to have some control over one's own priorities is an advantage. This will also allow the individual to practice a sense of responsibility and commitment to see the success of their real estate incursion.

There are also some very good tax advantages in using real estate to get an orderly residual income base. This can be reflected in the system that is currently used to encourage the active sale of real estate. Thus by providing the necessary tax breaks,

the person is more likely to work even harder to achieve a comfortable residual income goal.

Diversifying the ability to earn residual income without the hassle of having to establish a separate company or organization is a better option to consider, since real estate incursion does not really require these facilities.

 PASSIVE INCOME

Use of blogs

The use of this method in order to obtain residual income is a necessity at this time. For those who are Internet connoisseurs, this is an excellent way to stay in the business of creating residual income for yourself.

Thinking that having a certain level of experience is necessary, is not absolute as everyone has to start somewhere. Learning to use the best available techniques to create successful blogs will directly relate to the amount of residual income derived.

Web Logs

In order to achieve a fairly lucrative residual income from blogs there must be a certain amount of commitment. The success of blogs depends largely on the individual's level of interest and ability to search for relevant information in order to ensure that the blogs made are interesting and captivating.

Focusing on the promotional aspect of blogs will ensure the exposure necessary for the

 PASSIVE INCOME

blog to be as visited as possible. Promoting one's own content on a social networking website and leaving the relevant information on the website will ensure that the blog is well connected. This is also creating the highest percentages required when there is more traffic generated through referral sites.

Posting ads on the person's blog will also provide a source of income, as the person is in a position to charge for the ads.

This only applies if the traffic to such a blog site is a lot, therefore, there will be many other people or companies willing to pay for appearing as ads on the blog site, with the intention that they in turn bring traffic to their sites as well.

 PASSIVE INCOME

Getting other people to write interesting things that are then presented on the individual's own blog is a very good way to keep the blog interesting and diversified.

 PASSIVE INCOME

Set goals and have a plan

Plans and objectives go hand in hand, without one the other is redundant.

Having these two elements very present in a person's life is the key to staying focused on getting better living conditions at every step into the future.

 PASSIVE INCOME

Some suggestions

In most scenarios money plays an important role in being the motivating factor that pushes the individual. The motivation levels of an individual are, in fact, what drives the effort to the levels of success achieved.

As most people today are looking for easier ways to make money, the birth of many new efforts seem to be almost daily. More and more creative ways are being devised with the main intention of making money as fast and as fast as possible.

Once an individual has decided on a goal, the next step would be to devise an appropriate plan to achieve it successfully. Points such as marketability, levels of commitment, financial investments, labor are just some of the things that need to be taken into account when making plans.

Deadlines are also another very important issue to take into account when making plans to reach the target. Most targets can be achieved with some degree of commitment, but to ensure that the initial enthusiasm is not lost, an appropriate timeframe must be established. This will not only ensure that the objective is achieved, but will also keep the individual focus on achieving it quickly.

Taking the time to seriously consider the individual's ambitions will help to get a clearer idea of what the objectives and plans should be. Identifying this is the most important thing to ensure that the plan and goals are worked on and successfully completed. Knowing one's own capabilities and being realistic in deciding objectives and plans is also a way to be wise and prudent.

PASSIVE INCOME

The mentality necessary for a passive income

Those who have successfully ventured into the passive income style of creating an income for themselves have realized that

PASSIVE INCOME

they have a very different mentality than the average individual.

These people are usually driven by ambition and money and will do their best to achieve both. In seeking to achieve the desired residual income through passive means, the individual needs to be willing to try any kind of effort.

What you need

Generally, the individual who chooses to provide residual income for himself through the passive income style are people who are very focused and with a positive mindset. The strong positive mood is almost a prerequisite for keeping the individual on the path to success.

 PASSIVE INCOME

Being hopeful is also another attribute that is needed for this kind of effort. Because this residual income style does not have the pressure of having to respond to superiors for not achieving a certain amount of business, the individual has to have all the positive attributes necessary to be able to push himself to the next level.

This is especially necessary when energy levels are low and along with the fact that there may be a lack of visible achievements that are evident.

Final thoughts

There are many entrepreneurs who have chosen to venture into such income arrears. Most of them already have the drive and goal of being a success firmly in place and all they need is to be able to identify the relevant effort that will provide what they want.

They are always alert to any possible avenue that will allow them to create a healthy residual income scenario. Being always aware will also ensure that they are well aware of the possibilities available to them.

 PASSIVE INCOME

Visit our author page on Amazon and get more MENTES LIBRES!

http://amazon.com/author/menteslibres

If you wish, you can leave a comment on this book by clicking on the following link so that we can continue to grow! Thank you very much for your purchase!

https://www.amazon.com/dp/B082RGZ3Q3

www.ingramcontent.com/pod-product-compliance
Lightning Source LLC
Chambersburg PA
CBHW040248220526

45473CB00001B/408